THREE BOOKS — ONE EDUCATIONAL EDITION

STORY ONE *Her Story*, STORY TWO *Pula's Vacation*, & STORY THREE

The World of Sports According to Pula

Pula

By "Princess"

Illustrated By Ann Tango-Schurmann

To order additional copies of this book, contact:
Xlibris
1-888-795-4274
www.Xlibris.com
Orders@Xlibris.com

ISBN: 978-1-4134-8923-1 (sc)
ISBN: 978-1-4134-8924-8 (hc)

Library of Congress Control Number: 2005902047

Print information available on the last page

Rev. date: 09/30/2019

Dedicated to my parents

Frank & Fedora

who gave birth to my creativity

and to my husband Angel who

encouraged its development

Illustrated By Ann Tango-Schurmann
Layout By Kristin Belger

Pula

STORY ONE

Her Story

Lessons in Creative Writing, Art and Geography

By "Princess"

Hello — my name is Pula!

What is your name?

Write it here_____.

I am a pink flamingo — *that is a type of bird.*

I bet that you are a boy *or* girl.

Put a check in the box next to which one you are.

☐ Boy

☐ Girl

I was born in Miami Beach, Florida.

Where were you born?

Write it here_____.

My mother is a Princess.

My father is an Angel.

On the next page I want you to draw a picture

of what your mother and father look like.

Draw your parents on this page.

Very Good!

I used to go to Middle School. My mother was a teacher there. I had many friends. They wrote lots of stories about me. There were stories about my trip to Paris.

Where do you take trips?

Write it here_____.

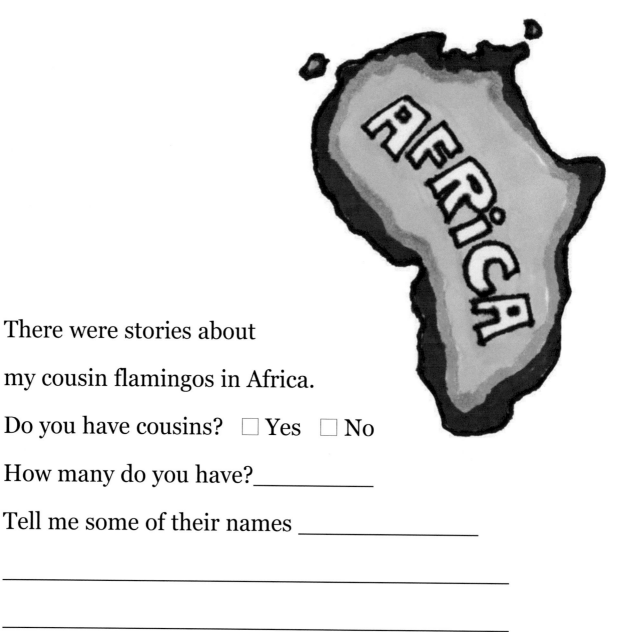

There were stories about

my cousin flamingos in Africa.

Do you have cousins? ☐ Yes ☐ No

How many do you have?_____

Tell me some of their names _____

_____

_____

_____

_____

Wow!

There were stories about my wedding to Johnny.

There were even stories about my baby girl

flamingo — Gardenia Elizabeth.

I am going to tell you the story about my wedding in Paris, France to Johnny.

It all began with my engagement to Johnny on Valentine's Day of 2000. My mom and dad gave me a very nice party in Miami Beach at the Fountainpink Hotel. There were many people there and we had fun.

I bet that you like parties. Do you have many birthday parties?   ☐ Yes   ☐ No

*W*ell — after the party, in April my mom and dad took me back to Paris, France. I really like Paris. I used to go there a lot when I was a little girl flamingo.

We left New York on a beautiful sunny Sunday, and arrived in Paris on Monday in the morning. We went straight to my favorite place — the Eiffel Tower — then to Notre Dame Cathedral — and then to the Louvre Museum.

At Notre Dame, I met my cousin
Slappy from Africa with her
husband Danny Bird and their children.
They were going to visit Disneyland,
Magic Kingdom in Paris.

Have you ever visited any of the Disney parks?

☐ Yes   ☐ No

I was so excited that I told mom and dad that I
wanted to get married to Johnny in Paris at
Notre Dame. So, we e-mailed Johnny and his
mom in Miami Beach and asked them what they
thought about the idea. They were very happy
and flew over.

Use my photo below, and dress me as a bride!

Creative Hints:
a. Draw wedding clothes.
b. Cut out paper and glue.
c. Clip fabric and paste.
d. Use your imagination!

Don't forget my veil!

16

That looks great — Thank You!

On the morning of April 29, 2000 — I married
Johnny at Notre Dame Cathedral. I wore a
beautiful gown like the one that you just drew.
Slappy was my matron of honor and she wore
a pink silk gown.

Were you ever in a wedding? ☐ Yes   ☐ No

Then, Johnny and I went to the French Riviera to
honeymoon on our yacht. We have a happy life
and many more stories. *Au Revior* for now
— that means "Bye, Bye" in French.

MANY THANKS

Muchas Gracias

To

Angel, Pula's Dad

Aunt (*Tía*) Libby & Aunt (*Tía*) Mary Jo,

Gardenia's Spanish Tutors,

The State Department of Education

Core Curriculum Standards

that inspired the creation

of Pula.

Illustrated By Ann Tango-Schurmann

Layout By Kristin Belger

Pula

STORY TWO

Pula's Vacation

Little Spanish and Travel Lessons for Gardenia
Christmas in the Caribbean

By "Princess"

Hello!

In my last storybook (el libro), I told you about my wedding to Johnny and the birth of my daughter (la hija), Gardenia. Since then, I gave birth to twin boys (los muchachos) — Nickkie and Frankkie. It is very unusual for flamingos to have two (dos) babies at one time. This makes my sons (los hijos) very important (muy importante).

Did you know that flamingo chicks have gray (gris) or white (blanco) feathers until they are one (uno) or two (dos) years old?

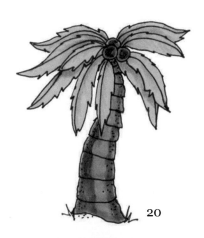

Without eating food containing carotene — an orange pigment — their feathers cannot become pink (rosado) or red (rojo). So, even baby chicks have to eat foods like carrots!

I am happy (contenta) to have you join me for another story (el cuento). This time we are going to learn a few words in Spanish (Español). Johnny and I are taking Gardenia to the Caribbean for Christmas (Navidad) to visit family (la familia). Johnny's great-grandma was from Cuba. So Gardenia, Nickkie and Frankkie have a lot of relatives (los parientes) there.

*B*efore we go, Gardenia has to learn a few important words in Spanish. I bet that you will be learning a foreign language when you go to school (la escuela). My sons (los hijos) are too young to make the long trip (el viaje). They will stay with Johnny's mom (la madre) in Miami Beach. She is their grandmother (la abuela) and they love her very much.

Please (por favor) draw a picture (el cuadro) of your favorite family (la familia) member besides your parents.

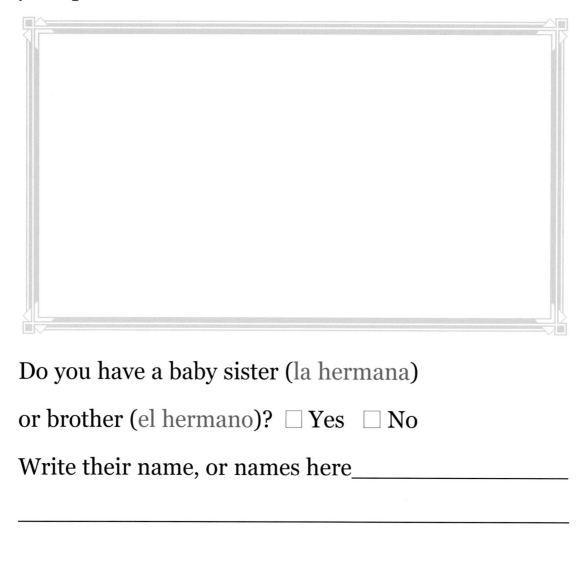

Do you have a baby sister (la hermana)

or brother (el hermano)? ☐ Yes ☐ No

Write their name, or names here_____

_____

_____

You are doing very well.
Now (ahora), let us continue.

Pula wants Gardenia to become familiar

with a few words in the Spanish language.

Here are just a few. Maybe you can suggest to

Pula some other words. If so, write them on the

bottom of this page, either in English or Spanish.

Thank you very much (muchas gracias)!

school	la escuela	orange	la naranja
doctor	el médico	apple	la manzana
airplane	el avión	grandfather	el abuelo
boat	el barco	grandmother	la abuela
island	la isla	uncle	el tío
ocean	el océano	aunt	la tía
sun	el sol	cousin (boy)	el primo
sea	el mar	cousin (girl)	la prima
day	el día	picture	el cuadro
hour	la hora	milk	la leche
dog	el perro	chocolate	el chocolate
fisherman	el pescador	kitchen	la cocina
dress	el vestido		

Can you use these words and write a Spanish story?

Try it.

THE BODY — EL CUERPO

Please (por favor) draw a line to my body parts.

eye
el ojo

head
la cabeza

mouth
la boca

leg
la pierna

neck
el cuello

foot
el pie

Please (por favor) place YOUR PHOTO on this page.

Now, label the parts just like you did with
Pula. Look at Pula again to remember all the
Spanish words.

THE DAYS OF THE WEEK
LOS DÍAS DE LA SEMANA

What is today (hoy)?

Please (por favor) check the box next to the day below.

☐	Monday	lunes	☐ Friday	viernes
☐	Tuesday	martes	☐ Saturday	sábado
☐	Wednesday	miércoles	☐ Sunday	domingo
☐	Thursday	jueves		

THE MONTHS OF THE YEAR
LOS MESES DEL AÑO

Please (por favor) check your birthday (el cumpleaños) month below.

☐	January	enero	☐ July	julio
☐	February	febrero	☐ August	agosto
☐	March	marzo	☐ September	septiembre
☐	April	abril	☐ October	octubre
☐	May	mayo	☐ November	noviembre
☐	June	junio	☐ December	diciembre

¡Muy Bien!

NUMBERS — NÚMEROS

Please (por favor) check the box next to your age.

		English	Español			English	Español
☐	1	One	Uno/Una	☐	6	Six	Seis
☐	2	Two	Dos	☐	7	Seven	Siete
☐	3	Three	Tres	☐	8	Eight	Ocho
☐	4	Four	Cuatro	☐	9	Nine	Nueve
☐	5	Five	Cinco	☐	10	Ten	Diez

Use these numbers to count from 1-10 in Spanish and then continue with English to complete the dot-to-dot picture.

FLAMINGO FACTS

id you know?

- Flamingos can live in many places. There are flamingos in the Caribbean islands, parts of Asia, Africa, South America, and here in North America they can be found in zoos and animal parks (el parque — the park).

- Flamingos like to eat worms, insects, small shellfish, and tiny green plants. They use their bills to filter the food (la comida) out of the water.

    - It takes 28 (veintiocho) days for a flamingo to be born. It is very unusual for them to lay more than one (uno) egg (el huevo) at a time.

Please (por favor) use your favorite colors to color Pula.

COLORS — LOS COLORES

Please (por favor) check your favorite color.

☐ Yellow   Amarillo   ☐ Pink   Rosado
☐ Blue   Azul   ☐ Purple   Violeta
☐ Red   Rojo   ☐ Orange   Anaranjado
☐ Green   Verde   ☐ Black   Negro

LET'S COOK PULA'S FAVORITE RECIPE
VAMOS A COCINAR

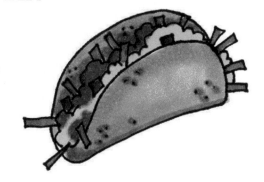

Pula's Taco Delight

1 lb. (la libra) of chopped meat (la carne)

1 jar of salsa

1 package (el paquette) of shredded cheddar cheese

Lettuce (la lechuga)

Chopped tomato (el tomate)

5 (cinco) taco shells

4 (cuatro) tablespoons of oil

Pre-heat oven — 350 degrees

Brown meat in oil, add salsa and cook for 5 (cinco) minutes.
Place mixture in taco shells, add cheese and bake in oven for
10 (diez) minutes. Remove and add lettuce (la lechuga)
and tomato (el tomate). Sit down at your table (la mesa)
and enjoy! You will not even need to use a knife
(el cuchillo), fork (el tenedor), or spoon (la cuchara).
Remember to use your napkin (la servilleta)!

Enjoy!

FOODS — LOS ALIMENTOS

Please (por favor) check your favorite foods below.

☐ egg — el huevo

☐ fish — el pescado

☐ ice cream — el helado

☐ cheese — el queso

☐ soup — la sopa

☐ cake — el pastel

☐ bread — el pan

☐ salad — la ensalada

☐ meat — la carne

ow, using the color chart below, draw a line from the color in each flag (la bandera) to the color written in center.

United States of America

red — rojo

blue — azul

white — blanco

Cuba

You know all about Pula's vacation, and Gardenia's lessons.

Tell us in the space provided below:

- How many new words have you learned, both English and Spanish, from the story?

- Where would you like to go on vacation?

Wherever you go — Have a Great Time!

My Vacation

◯ _____
_____
_____
_____
_____
_____
_____
_____
_____
◯ _____
_____
_____
_____
_____

Illustrated By Ann Tango-Schurmann
Layout By Kristin Belger

Pula

The World of Sports
According to Pula

Lessons in Physical Education,
Math and Cooking

By "Princess"

Hello!

Welcome back to my story. We left off with Spanish lessons for my daughter — Gardenia — and our family vacation to the Caribbean. Now, it is time to *tackle* the job of lessons in sports for my twin chicks — Nickkie and Frankkie.

When raising boy chicks, it is important for their dad to know a lot about sports. Although, the language can be confusing at times.

For example, the word *tackle*. It can be used just as I did — meaning to get a job done. But it, can also be used in football, meaning the act of stopping. In fishing, it describes the equipment used to fish.

Johnny, their dad, is so busy running the family enterprises, that he doesn't have time for lessons in sports. My Dad Angel was a star basketball player and grew up with many sport legends. As for Mommy Princess, she still isn't all grown-up — but, we love her. Her main sport is shopping!

Here are some short clips from the "mini-sport" camp that Grandpa Angel held for Nickkie and Frankkie.

Lesson ONE
BASKETBALL

There are 5 players on a team. They run up and down the court and try to put the basketball in the hoop. If they are successful, they get 2 points. If it is a really long shot, they get 3 points. Now, you don't want to *foul* anyone. Because by not playing by the rules of the game, you can get in trouble. Notice the word *foul* is not *fowl*, like a flamingo and other types of birds.

Lesson TWO
BASEBALL

This is the "All American" sport. It is played with 9 players on a field called a *diamond*. Gardenia likes baseball because she thinks that the players get to play on a huge — really BIG — *diamond* like my engagement ring! "That's not the same type of *diamond*, Gardenia." However, if the team wins the World Series, they do get huge rings with lots of *diamonds* and other precious stones on them.

Lesson THREE
GOLF

You can play golf all by yourself or with as many as 3 other players on your team. You use a little white ball and iron clubs. Many women prefer to use multi-colored balls such as "flamingo" pink! People go around a large piece of land called a golf course. It has 18-holes and each hole can be either worth 3, 4 or 5 points. They have to get the ball in the hole with as few hits as possible. In fact, if they get the ball in the hole on a 3-point hole, with only 2 hits, they get a *birdie*. When Nickkie and Frankkie heard this, they became very upset.

They thought that people tried to catch birds like us or our cousins — ducks, swans, and geese! Grandpa decided not to go into the reasons that people get eagles! Do you know? Grandpa did tell them to be careful, if they do decide to play golf and to duck when people yell "4"! It doesn't mean that they got a great score — instead it means that their ball is about to hit you!

*L*esson FOUR
TENNIS

Love used in tennis means

that you don't have any points.

Not like the *love* that you have for

your family! There are so many words in

sports that really can get little chicks and

children confused. Anyway, tennis is played

on a court but not the same type as basketball.

The players have to get the ball over the net

but not the same type of net used in fishing

or basketball! You can play with 1 other player

or 3 other players.

The "mini-sport" camp proved a little too much for the twins. They decided to just go fishing with their Uncle Danny Bird. "Just fishing," yelled Grandpa Angel. He then proceeded to tell them that fishing is a very difficult sport. If you want to do it correctly, you must know a lot about science, geography, math, engineering and many other educational things. There are almost as many types of fishing as there are fish! But for now, Grandpa Angel told them that they could just get their little poles and go down to the pond. The twins put away their golf clubs, basketballs, baseballs and all the other equipment that they had collected for camp.

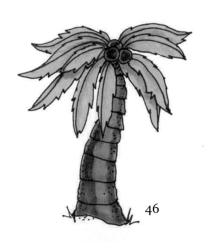

They never got to hockey, ice skating, soccer, and all the other great sports. After all, Grandpa Angel and Daddy Johnny have to realize that the twins are only 5 years old!

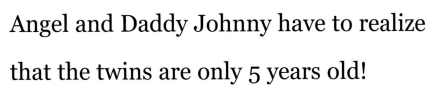

If you haven't noticed yet, all sports are a "numbers game". So let's talk numbers. The twins want you to circle all the numbers in this story. Then, they want you to add them up.

Put the answer here on this line _____. Then subtract your age. Put the answer here on this line _____. By the way, how old are you? Put it on this line _____.

Thank you for being a good sport!

Write your favorite sport, or sports, down on this page. Tell us a little sport story about yourself. Who taught you about the sport? You can learn a lot of good sport stuff from adults, but reading books can, also, be helpful.

_____

_____

_____

_____

_____

_____

_____

_____

_____

_____

_____

_____

_____

_____

Before you go, please draw a "prize" fish and a boat for the twins. Yes, you guessed it. The twins really want to fish. They are even willing to learn all that it will take to be good fishermen. So, as they grow, Uncle Danny Bird will have his hands full. I wonder if it is the fish or Uncle Danny Bird's beautiful boat.

Do you have any "fishtails"
for us? If you do, write
about them below.

_____

_____

_____

_____

_____

_____

_____

_____

_____

_____

_____

_____

_____

_____

_____

_____

_____

_____

_____

_____

By Nickkie and Frankkie

Johnny and I have Chef Charles on our yacht to do all of our cooking. Don't you know that our twin boy chicks decided to give chef some advice!

Here is their tuna recipe. No, not tuna salad — fresh tuna from the sea!

Take one big piece of tuna, in grown-up measurement, that is about 2 inches thick. Place it in a baking dish with some olive oil. Cover the tuna with Dijon mustard. We live in France, so the boys are very familiar with the town of Dijon. Then, sprinkle the top of the tuna with chopped nuts. They love walnuts. What type of nuts do you like to eat? Bake for 20 minutes at 350 degrees, and then broil on low for 5 minutes. Besides sports, cooking has a lot of numbers, too.

Chef Charles, Johnny and myself have to admit that the tuna was awesome! We really think that Uncle Danny Bird had a lot to do with the recipe. Oh, wait! Gardenia wants equal time. While we were in the Caribbean, Tía Elisabetta Rossina taught her a really good recipe.

Cook and skin a BIG red pepper. Fill it with ricotta cheese, smoked whiting, muenster cheese, and oregano. Cover it with salsa and bake it in the oven in a covered dish for 20 minutes at 350 degrees. It is really good. Oh, by the way — you can stuff as many peppers as you want, one for each member of your family.

I guess with the children cooking, the rest of us can relax. Think again! Nanny Nicole must be with them in the kitchen at all times. No chick or child should ever be left alone to cook without an adult! Safety first is very important, whether playing, cooking, or walking to school.

Gone Fishing — The End

Printed in the United States
By Bookmasters